Educating for Life

A Spiritual Vision
for Every Teacher and Parent

THE HANDBOOK

Thomas H. Groome

ThomasM
– An RCL Con

Allen, Te.

Send all inquiries to:
Thomas More®
An RCL Company
200 East Bethany Drive
Allen, Texas 75002-3804

Toll Free 800–888–3065
Fax 800–688–8356

Printed in the United States of America

ISBN 0–88347–366–6

1 2 3 4 5   02 01 00 99 98

Table of Contents

INTRODUCTION

Handbook

The purpose of this handbook is to advance the discussion about educating *for life for all*. This guide—which includes 10 sessions, one for each chapter of the book—may be used by administrators, faculties, school/parent groups and teachers or parents meeting in parish religious education programs. Offering a multilevel approach, the first part of the handbook features a *Recap* of each chapter along with the *For Reflection* exercises and questions that are featured in *Educating for Life*. Since both are an integral part of the book, they deserve to be probed and analyzed.

The handbook includes *Additional Reflections*, a *Concluding Thought*, and a *Glossary*. The recommended time for each of the 10 sessions is 90 minutes; 60 minutes for the *Reflection* section and about 30 minutes for the other exercises.

Since *Educating for Life* is geared toward teachers and parents, addressing both as educators, the handbook is designed to include educational as well parenting questions. To get maximum benefit from the book, each participant in the discussion groups should have their own copy of the book and handbook. In fact, the handbook also serves as a personal journal. Writing is a process by which we discover and clarify what lives in us. That is why keeping an *Educating for Life* journal is so effective. It reveals the deepest values that pervade the life of education while highlighting the crucial issues educators and parents face. It also serves as a memory log that can be referred to again and again—and updated accordingly.

CHAPTER ONE

A Promise to Educators: "To Shine Like the Stars of Heaven"

Recap

Regardless of what teachers and parents teach, they instruct *people*, and the better they do so the more they influence the whole person—head, heart, and hands. To be an educator is to stand on holy ground—people's lives. (page 35)

Consider the worthiest purpose of education is that learners might become fully alive human beings who help to create a society that serves the common good. (page 36)

This book's intent is to give parents and teachers—regardless of religious persuasion—access to the rich spiritual reservoir of Catholic Christianity as a resource to their own philosophical and spiritual foundations. (page 40)

Research shows that the following characteristics lend distinctiveness to U.S. Catholic schools:

- They provide a holistic curricula that embraces the totality of the person—intellectual, moral, social, aesthetic, physical, and spiritual.

- They have a significant "social capital" of support provided by the sponsoring faith community.

- They offer a structured curricula with emphasis on core studies in the liberal arts and a strong commitment to academic rigor.

- Good collegiality exists among faculty and staff, with broad commitment to forging the schools into caring communities.

- Their decentralized governance makes them more responsive to local needs. "Virtually all important decision are made at individual school sites."

- In a concerted effort, they nurture social consciousness in students through justice activities, with outreach and service to the local community—especially people in need.

- They have a compelling spiritual vision shared by faculty, staff, and parents. (page 51)

The core characteristics of Catholic Christianity are:

- Its positive anthropology—a benevolent or caritas understanding of the human condition;

- Its conviction about the sacramentality of life—that there is always "the more" to be found in the ordinary and everyday;

- Its emphasis on relationship and community—the conviction that humankind is "made for each other;"

- Its commitment to history and tradition—honoring the legacy of wisdom, arts, and sciences, including the Scriptures and traditions of Christian faith left by generations before us; and

- Its appreciation of a wisdom rationality—favoring a reflective way of knowing that encourages responsibility and wisdom for life.

Three other substantial characteristics permeate the life of Catholicism:

They are an emphasis on:

- spirituality—on seeking "holiness" of life.
- working for justice and the social values of God's reign.
- catholicity itself—hospitality for all and, as St. Augustine emphasized, being open to truth wherever it can be found. (pages 59–60)

For Reflection (60 minutes)

1. Take a few moments to write down your own sense of what it means to be educator as a parent or teacher. "Being an educator means . . ." Then reflect on what or who has influenced your understanding.

2. Defining educator very broadly (e.g., as in the opening story—your mom), recall some of the great ones you have encountered. Dwell in the memory of them again. What phrase or metaphor might describe their vision of education?

3. What can you learn from such great educators for your own vocation as teacher or parent?

4. Take a few moments and jot down some associations that emerge for you when you hear the word Catholic.

5. Uncover the story behind your associations. Where do they come from? Which are stereotypes? Which seem authentic?

6. What are some implications of the authentic characteristics of Catholic Christianity for teachers or parents?

7. What seems most important for you to take away from this opening chapter?

8. Is there a decision or sense of renewed opportunity emerging for you?

Additional Reflections (30 minutes)

The rest of the story . . . Tell a story from your experience about the best educator you have ever encountered. Jot down and discuss what you learned about the art of teaching from that person.

_____

_____

_____

_____

1. How do good teachers influence the whole person—head, heart, and soul?

2. Explain: Educators are in need of affirmation? Why are educators—teachers and parents—"easy targets" for the media? Do stories about good educators and good parents attract high/low interest?

3. What is your philosophy about "educational results?" How do you define and measure them? Do you expect immediate results in your classroom/home?

4. My spiritual vision of education is

   _____

   _____

5. My spiritual vision of parenting is

   _____

   _____

6. How does your spiritual vision enable people to become fully alive? Like Plato, do you see yourself "turning the soul" of learners?

7. On a scale of 1 to 5 (5 = very strong), rank and discuss how well your overall school or program exemplifies each of the characteristics. Repeat the same exercise for your specific classroom. Also give at least one example of how your specific context exemplifies any one of the following characteristics.

- A positive understanding of the human condition.
- A conviction about the sacramentality of life.
- A sense of community—humankind is meant for each other.
- A commitment to history and tradition.
- An appreciation for the wisdom for life.
- An effort to seek holiness of life.
- A willingness to work for justice.
- A commitment to hospitality for all.

8. My teaching style influences the heads, hearts, and souls of learners because

_____

_____

_____

_____

_____

_____

_____

_____

_____

_____

_____

_____

Concluding Thought

"The process of saying "yes" to God is spirituality."
—*Lawrence Cunningham*

Some of the "yeses" in my spiritual vision of education are:

_____

_____

_____

_____

Glossary

ontology—a branch of metaphysics concerned with the nature and relations of being.

metaphysics—a division of philosophy that tries to assemble clear ideas that are true of every aspect of ultimate reality.

anthropology—the science and philosophy that delves into the origin, nature, and destiny of human beings.

collegiality—the equal sharing of authority.

Christian spirituality—Christian life guided and empowered by the Holy Spirit and following "the way" of Jesus.

reign of God—the dynamic action of God's saving power that brings about God's intentions of "fullness of life."

CHAPTER TWO

A Good People: "God's Own Image and Likeness"

Recap

Regardless of philosophy, the fact remains that every teacher and parent—indeed, every person—has a "functioning anthropology," whether we advert to it or not. In other words, we have a working sense of our own "selves" and an opinion of others. This general perspective on "the human condition" shapes our way of life, our way of relating to self, others, and the world—our entire *modus operandi* as human beings. (pages 70–71)

The correlation of anthropology, education, and politics becomes self-evident when we recognize that all social injustices are undergirded by erroneous anthropologies. What else are racism, sexism, and ethnocentrism but ideologies that certain people are more human than others and, therefore, the "others" need not be accorded the dignity and rights due to full human beings? (page 73)

The Catholic Christian disposition is to embrace one's humanness as gift, to celebrate it as essentially good, to relish its joys, to be tolerant of its imperfections and merciful when one sins. (page 75)

Teachers and parents need a bedrock attitude that affirms the essential goodness and giftedness of people . . . . [they] should also be able to see great possibilities in people . . . . . [and] regardless of where, what, who, or how they teach, are entrusted to educate the character of learners to fulfill responsibilities corresponding to their rights. This means forming them to be deeply committed to promoting a decent quality of life for everyone. (pages 94–102)

For Reflection (60 minutes)

1. Take time to jot down "my own understanding of the human condition." Free-associate and notice what emerges. (Caution: Do not overlook "the obvious" about us—it could be most significant.)

2. Reviewing your own sense of yourself, uncover some of the background that has shaped your anthropology— influential people, significant experiences, cultural conditions. Note the insights that emerge.

3. Think now of some consequences your functioning anthropology has for how you educate.

4. From your experience, think of one notable situation in which a positive anthropology was working. Then think of an instance where a negative one was dominant. What do you learn from each instance for your own educating?

5. Imagine some likely consequences if you approach your teaching with a consistently positive anthropology.

6. What are some roadblocks that you experience to implementing a humanitas anthropology? Think of deterrents inside and outside of yourself, both psychological and in your social context.

7. Given how crucial an educator's anthropology is for teaching, what new insights have emerged for you from the chapter? What would you add to its proposals?

8. How do you describe the core consequences for education of a *humanitas* anthropology? What are you coming to see for yourself as asked of your soul, of your style, and of the educational space you help to create?

9. Are there any particular decisions that you feel drawn to by this chapter?

Additional Reflections (30 minutes)

The rest of the story . . .Tell a story from your experience about a situation in which someone maintained trust and acceptance in you in the midst of disapproval by others. What do you learn from this story about the power of continuing support and acceptance from someone? How does the example of that person help you to this day through the ups and downs of life?

1. The "operating anthropology" of the learners and the educator (what they really think about humankind) is

   _____
   _____
   _____

2. How do class reunions and school yearbooks uniquely recall the "functioning anthropology" of your school experiences?

3. When you were in school what was your impression of former students visiting their former teacher? Have you ever visited former teachers? For what reasons? How does this reflect the "functioning anthropology" of the specific teachers involved?

4. What are the positive anthropologies operating in your classroom, program or home that expose racism, sexism, and violence for what they are?

5. My teaching/parenting style and classroom/home atmosphere convey a "realistic optimism" about the human condition in these ways:

   _____

   _____

   _____

6. On a scale of 1 to 5 (5 = very strong), rank and discuss how well your school, home or program exemplifies each of these aspects of a Christian anthropology. Repeat the same exercise for your specific classroom. Also, give at least one example of how your school/classroom express a Christian anthropology.

   • People are essentially good and dignified though capable of sin.

   • Our body and soul are not separate entities; this divine life in humankind gives us a homing instinct for God.

   • We become fully a person through relationship and community.

   • We have a responsibility to care for neighbor and for the common good.

   • Our human potential is boundless.

   • By God's design, we have a sense of right and wrong.

   • To be human is to choose, to decide, to chart our own course, and to make a difference in history.

   • We are made from love and for loving.

   • Our lives have an eternal destiny.

7. Rank in order of importance (from most important to less important) these attitudes and commitments of the

teacher's/parent's heart. What attitudes and commitments would you add to this list?

- I affirm the innate goodness of the learner.
- I see great possibilities in every person.
- I encourage learners to be initiators and creators who can make a difference.
- I reach out to the whole learner—physical gifts, moral gifts, and spiritual gifts.
- I help my students/children live with freedom, respect human rights, and to fulfill responsibilities.

8. What are some ways you create a respectful environment in your classroom or home? How well do your students/children value their own ideas and feelings? How well do they listen to and respect the ideas and feelings of one another?

9. How do you maintain a balance between challenging learners to excel and yet not create an atmosphere of unhealthy competition?

⋘◇⋙

_____

_____

_____

_____

_____

_____

_____

_____

_____

_____

_____

Concluding Thought

"There is no one alive who is you-er than you."
                                                —Dr. Seuss

Some of my unique talents and gifts are:

_____

_____

_____

_____

My teaching style/parenting style fosters the unique talents and gifts of others when

_____

_____

_____

_____

Glossary

soul—a person's animating and defining principle.

postmodernist—relating to a movement that is a reaction against modern philosophy, and especially its overconfidence in reason and absolute truths.

philosophy—the literal meaning in Greek is "love of wisdom."

theology—the literal meaning in Greek is "the science of God."

sociology—the systematic study of organized groups of human beings.

CHAPTER THREE

A Gracious World: "Seeing God in All Things"

Recap

In our efforts to make sense of the world, we notice that all is not rosy! This is not a perfect place—far from it. The renowned philosopher and theologian Bernard Lonergan writes of the world of meaning that is organized by intelligence, that is described by language, that is enriched by tradition. It is an enormous world far beyond comprehension of the nursery. But it is also "an insecure world, for besides fact there is fiction, besides truth there is error, besides science there is myth, besides honesty there is deceit." (page 122)

Good education can help change a person's worldview, but better by far that teachers and parents help learners to put in place a *for life for all* outlook from the beginning. An educator who sees the world predominantly as threatening will, even unconsciously, encourage learners to live defensively. A teacher or parent who sees life as a gift will teach an outlook of gratitude toward the world. (pages 123–124)

No greater claim can be made for the world than that it is the ordinary medium of God's outreach to humankind and of human response to God. A world so good as to be sacramental, pointing to it as gracious, meaningful, and worthwhile, is the core of the Catholic Christian attitude toward the world. I will call it a sacramental cosmology. (page 125)

I suggest that the particular fulcrum of a sacramental cosmology is people's imagination. Imagination is key for at least two reasons: first, to "see" the "more" in the midst of the ordinary; and second, to perceive what ought to be and have motivation to act accordingly. (page 132)

A sacramental outlook on life in the world reflects at least two convictions in faith: (a) that God takes the initiative to reach out to humankind in the world and enters into partnership with us—enters into a covenant—and (b) that God's intentions toward humankind are gracious. God's sentiment for the world is abiding LOVE. (page 136)

For Reflection (60 minutes)

1. Take a few notes on "my basic outlook on life." List some of dominant features and favors.

2. Drawing the leading characteristics together and, on a scale of 1 to 10 (10 being most positive), give yourself an overall rating. Are you happy with your score? Why or why not?

3. Review and summarize your general responses to a sacramental cosmology. What do you agree with, disagree with? What would you add as a recommendation by way of worldview?

4. What do you imagine are some implications for education? For the parent/educator's own soul? For style of teaching? For the educational space a teacher or a parent helps to create?

5. Note a few of your overall responses to this chapter. What do they help you to understand about your attitude toward life in the world?

6. If you were allowed only one decision in response to your dialogue with this chapter (you can, of course,

have as many as you wish), what would it be? Why? How would you begin to implement it the next time you find yourself in an educational moment?

Additional Reflections (30 minutes)

The rest of the story . . .Tell a story from your experience that has helped you to "see" the "more" in the midst of everyday life. Jot down and discuss how you pass on that sacramental outlook to learners.

_____

_____

_____

What do you think is the general tendency of young people: to look at the world as gracious place or as a foreboding place?

_____

_____

What underlies their basic worldview?

_____

_____

1. How do you enable sacramental moments to take place in your classroom, program or home?

2. My definition of sacrament is

   _____

   _____

3. What is sacramental consciousness? Given the wide range of home experiences (both good and bad), what do you consider the most crucial element in cultivating

in learners a positive attitude toward themselves, others, and God's creation? How do you encourage your students/children to live the grace of the sacraments, especially the Eucharist?

4. What is the role of liturgy in your school or home?

5. How do you cultivate the virtue of hope in learners—seeing the world as gracious and meaningful yet not ignoring suffering and evil? What kinds of things dampen hope in the lives of young people?

6. What are the most effective ways that teachers/parents can stimulate the sacramental imagination of young people—that is, helping them know and do what they ought to do?

7. What can parents/teachers do to make sure that sacramental practice is not naïve about evil and suffering? Does not become mechanical? Really nourishes faith?

8. Rank from most important to least important the attitudes that shape a sacramental outlook. Add attitudes that you consider essential to a realistic list. What are some factors and worldviews that work against fostering these attitudes?

- A positive outlook on life helps us live more humanly.

- We can see life as good and live it joyfully.

- We can approach life as gift.

- It is always possible to find "the more."

- The world is meaningful.

- Life is worthwhile.

- Life invites us to make the most of our unique gifts.

- To live well requires an act of faith.

9. Here are some ways that I develop the artistic talents of learners

_____

_____

Encourage their sense that life is worthwhile

_____

_____

Alert them to God's presence

_____

_____

Enliven their imaginations

_____

_____

Help them fulfill their responsibilities

_____

_____

Encourage their ecological awareness

_____

_____

❖

_____
_____
_____
_____
_____
_____
_____
_____
_____
_____

Educating for Life

Concluding Thought

"Our idea about God tells us more about ourselves than about God."

—Thomas Merton

My idea of God is:

_____

_____

These are some of the ways that God is reflected in my teaching/parenting style:

_____

_____

These are some of the things my idea of God reveals about my teaching/parenting style:

_____

_____

Glossary

cosmology—a branch of philosophy that deals with the nature of the universe and all created things.

CHAPTER FOUR

$\mathcal{A}$ *Community for Life:* "Made for Each Other"

Recap

Catholic Christianity has a substantial characteristic of communalism . . . . This communal emphasis in its ecclesiology—understanding of itself as a church—reflects and encourages a similar attitude toward society—the conviction that we live most humanly as a "community-of-persons" . . . . With dual emphasis on personal and social, Catholic Christianity affirms the dignity and rights of the person, and, at the same time, insists that humankind has an essentially communal nature—that we form societies by "nature" rather than by convenience or contract—and underscores people's responsibilities to society and society's responsibilities to all its members. (pages 174–175)

By noting the deepest and most authentic longings of the human heart, we get some inkling of what God intends and desires for humankind, such as: holiness and goodness, love and compassion, respect and responsibility, enjoyment and delight. (page 179)

A rather extraordinary symbol of Catholicism's insistence upon a community-of-persons ecclesiology—and thus sociology—was its reiteration at the Council of Trent of the "communion of saints and sinners" representing the somewhat radical notion that the community of faith reaches beyond the grave, that even death cannot break the bond of baptism. (page 187)

It would seem imperative, then, that educators/parents take great care about the language world they create by their teaching. With words their "tool-of-trade," likely nothing has more influence on learners than the language they use, the language patterns and exchanges they encourage. At a minimum, this requires teachers and parents to use language that affirms the dignity, equality, and value of all people. (page 197)

For Reflection (60 minutes)

1. How do you understand the relationship between the person and society? What are some responsibilities of each to the other?

2. To what extent do you think society shapes the character and identity of its individual members? Rate social influence on a scale of 1 (very low) to 10.

3 Try to figure out where your responses to these questions come from. Review especially the "sociology" of your responses, i.e., how has your own social context influenced your social perspective?

4. What has clarified your own operating sociology from dialogue with this chapter? What agreements or disagreements stand out? Any need for adjustment?

5. If an educator is committed to educating for a community-of-persons, what might this mean for one's soul? For teaching style? For the educational environment of home, school, or parish?

6. In your social context, what adjustments would a common-good perspective recommend?

7. Note some of the most significant insights that have emerged for you from your conversation with this chapter on sociology and ecclesiology?

8. What are some agreements you have with it? Additions you would make to its proposals?

9. Write a fresh definition of the social perspective that undergirds your own work as educator. Are there some particular decisions to which your summary invites you as teacher or parent?

Additional Reflections (30 minutes)

The rest of the story . . .Tell a story recalling a situation from your life that epitomizes an intense experience of community. Jot down and discuss what you consider to be the main ingredients of real community

_____

_____

My teaching style builds community because it emphasizes

_____

_____

1. What aspects of our society foster a sense of real community? A sense of individualism?

2. How effective is your school community/parish community/family community in helping you to find God? Serve the reign of God? Enhance the lives of one another?

3. In what way does the size of community (for instance, parish of 200 families vs. parish of 2000 families) foster a true sense and experience of being church?

4. My favorite saints are

_____

_____

They are examples of

_____

_____

_____

_____

I encourage learners to grow in holiness of life by

_____

_____

_____

_____

5. What are the essential elements that make a community a welcoming community? A Word of God community? A worshipping community? A community of service? A witnessing community?

6. Can anyone be truly educated without having cultivated the art of conversation? Listening skills? How do you make it possible for learners to develop the art of conversation?

7. Write a mission statement for Everysaint Parish (a mythical community of faith that truly prizes being a community of formation and transformation)

_____

_____

_____

_____

8. If you were designing the building plans for a new school, what physical details would you insist on in order to create an educational environment that is attuned to "living together as a community?"

9. What rituals of forgiveness do you celebrate in your classroom, home or parish? How does this help to bring about a deeper level of community?

10. As we enter the new millennium, what do you consider the greatest hope and promise for communities of faith?

_____

_____

_____

_____

The greatest obstacle?

_____

_____

_____

_____

❖

_____

_____

_____

_____

_____

_____

_____

_____

_____

_____

_____

_____

_____

❖

Concluding Thought

"Education is not the filling of a pail, but the lighting of a fire."
—*William Butler Yeats*

What are the day-by-day implications of approaching teaching/parenting on the basis of filling a pail/lighting a fire?

_____

_____

_____

What are some concrete differences that learners/children experience?

_____

_____

_____

In terms of visual images, how do you describe your approach to teaching/parenting?

_____

_____

_____

❖

Glossary

sociology—the study of social relationships, of people's assimilation into groups, and of the expectations people have of each other, and of their communities and social institutions.

ecclesiology —the theological study of the church.

koinonia—a welcoming community, the communion experienced by Christians.

kerygma—a word-of-God community, the act and the content of proclaiming the Good News of salvation.

leitourgia—a worshipping community, the public and official prayers and rites of the Church.

diakonia—a community of service, the work of building God's reign of peace and justice.

CHAPTER FIVE

A Tradition to Inherit:
"The Family Heirloom"

Recap

With an integrated sense of time, tradition becomes the past, present, and future combined, representing our whole time over time—that in which we dwell—leading to continuity and new direction. (page 220)

To honor a holistic sense of time, let teachers and parents adopt an attitude of critical appreciation toward tradition that would encourage learners to personally and discerningly appropriate its legacy as their own in the present—rather than passively inheriting or naively canonizing tradition—with each generation creatively renewing and amplifying its wisdom into the future. (page 221)

Catholicism's appreciation for tradition reflects its theology of revelation and particularly its conviction that human history is a medium of revelation—of religious knowing. (page 226)

Catholic education has continually reflected a deep bond between sacred and secular learning, between faith and culture. The partnership between revelation and reason, between faith and understanding—these convictions are present throughout the history of Catholic education . . . . Catholic Christianity has a similar appreciation for the arts. It includes them in its educational curriculum and has often been their patron, cherishing them for expressing the human reach for the transcendent. (page 232–233)

The best educators have passion for what they teach and teach it with integrity, but passion and integrity lend authority to any teacher and parent. (page 240)

Catholic Christianity understands tradition as a reliable source of wisdom, but far from stymieing reason, invites it; far from asking blind obedience, requires critical appropriation, far from arresting investigation, encourages it; far from posing anything as final, offers signposts and benchmarks of achievement to stimulate creativity and new life along the pilgrim way. (page 244)

In choosing what to teach in the curriculum of Christian religious education, it is imperative to keep in mind the purpose—what one is educating for: The tradition itself bears witness that the "intended learning outcome" of Christian religious education is *nurturing disciples of Jesus Christ, people who follow his "way" through a community of disciples—the Church—in the midst of the world.* (page 252)

For Reflection (60 minutes)

1. How would you describe your own philosophy of time? Of history? What are some implications for your work as teacher/parent?

2. On a scale of 1 (liability) to 10 (asset), how do you rate the value of tradition? Recall and review some of the "history"—personal or communal— behind your response.

3. With the poles being "traditionalist" and "iconoclast," where do you place yourself? Why?

4. Drawing together your reflections thus far, restate your own attitude toward "tradition."

5. Whatever your attitude may be, what does it imply for an educational curriculum?

6. What do you think tradition asks of the educator's heart? For the teaching style? For the educational environment?

7. What are some of your best insights from your conversation with this chapter?

8. Do you have disagreements with this chapter or adjustments to suggest?

9. Apropos tradition, are you reaching any decisions for your own vocation as teacher or parent?

Additional Reflections (30 minutes)

*The rest of the story . . .*Recall a story about a family tradition that you always looked forward to celebrating. In what way did celebrating that tradition put you in closer touch with your immediate family? Extended family? What do you enjoy most about preparing to celebrate family rituals and traditions?

_____

_____

_____

_____

1. In what way does our society have a bias against tradition? In what way does our society honor tradition? Does thinking for oneself nullify tradition?

2. How does a linear notion of time disconnect the past, present, and future? Are young people able to grasp "whole time"—the unity of past, present, and future?

3. What religious traditions nurture your identity? How do these traditions shape who you are? Serve as a source of vast strength?

4. How is the educational process a catalyst of God's reign?

5. How would your faith life change if you insisted that Divine Truth does not unfold through the great and small happenings of human life? That you do not have an innate capacity to recognize God's presence in your life? That biblical faith is not a living tradition?

6. What sort of teaching style helps to make tradition a great treasury of new life? Do young people have a tendency to look upon tradition as burdening baggage?

7. What kind of connection is there between appreciating the legacy of tradition and respecting people who celebrate those traditions?

8. In your own words, describe this concept: "Christian faith is to be lived and living, whole and wholesome." What do you think is the most important guideline for religious education?

9. As a Christian religious educator, how do you incorporate the metaphor of Story (the reality of Christian faith)/Vision (how Christian faith is to be lived) in your approach to passing on the faith tradition? How do Story and Vision enliven your own faith?

Concluding Thought

"The finest and boldest Christian effort, the freshest and most enduring, has always flourished from the roots of tradition."

—*Cardinal Henri de Lubac*

These are some ways that tradition gives life and vitality to the church for me

_____

_____

_____

Tradition helps me to look at my faith more imaginatively because

_____

_____

_____

Glossary

liberal—a leaning against tradition that assumes the new is always an improvement.

conservative—a static understanding of tradition that imposes norms for how things ought to be done now.

holistic—relating to complete systems and interacting wholes rather than a dissection of parts.

divine revelation—the self-disclosure of God.

culture—the sum total of social values reflected by a specific people at a specific period in history.

ecumenism—a process of bringing unity among all religious traditions.

CHAPTER SIX

A Reasonable Wisdom:
"Thinking for Life"

Recap

The Christian intellectual tradition reflects enduring commitment to knowing that unites the theoretical with the practical, knowledge with life, cognition with ethics. For the first thousand years of Christian education, this unity was warranted by the biblical tradition of wisdom. (page 280)

Scholastic philosophy and theology emerged around the beginning of the second millennium and has remained the dominant conceptual system of Roman Catholicism ever since . . . . Responding to its new context, theology became a "science" in quest of rational knowledge instead of prayerful contemplation seeking spiritual wisdom. (page 282)

The contemporary scholars I find most constructive in humanizing our ways of knowing—*for life for all*—are feminist epistemologists. In general, feminist epistemology focuses on gender bias in the dominant "ways of knowing"—how men are favored—and proposes a more inclusive and humanizing alternative from the perspective of women's experience. (page 284)

Biblically and philosophically, wisdom engages the while person, is located in time and place (in tradition and community), and encourages integrity between knower and knowledge, to become wise. (page 288)

Even without using religious language, educators can invite learners to reach beyond self- actualization—beyond "the self" as the measure of morality—toward universal ideals and values that are grounded in transcendence. I propose three great moral values that are "naturally" so persuasive, generic enough to suggest other more specific values, and powerful enough to lend real substance to character formation. The first two are companions, *respect* and *responsibility,* and then I add *compassion* to permeate the first two. (page 305)

For Reflection (60 minutes)

1. From your own experience, what does it entail to really "know" something?

2. Outline the process of obtaining such knowledge. In other words, how do you describe what philosophers call "the dynamics of cognition?"

3. When you teach, what is the most complete kind of "knowing" you intend people to reach? What difference do you hope such "knowing" will make in their lives?

4. Has your own sense of "knowledge" and of the "ways of knowing"—your epistemology—become any clearer from the previous reflections? In what ways? Why?

5. What do you imagine a wisdom epistemology asks of an educator's heart? Of how he or she teaches? Of the teaching/learning environment?

6. If you had one piece of advice to give young teachers or parents about their epistemology—how and what they want learners to know—what might you say?

7. What do you take away from this chapter on epistemology for your own educating? List three aspects that seem most significant to you.

8. Is there a concrete decision you want to make about "ways of knowing" and your own approach as a teacher or parent?

9. What adjustments would be needed to implement a wisdom epistemology in your school, parish program, or family?

Additional Reflections (30 minutes)

*The rest of the story . . .*Recall a story from your experience in which someone brought you to a breakthrough discovery. In a pithy statement, summarize the experience of seeing something new and fresh

_____

_____

_____

_____

1. What does it mean to be able to think for oneself and yet respect tradition? What are the necessary steps to keep both poles in balance?

2. What are some necessary practical aspects/theoretical aspects of a sound teaching style? Where do you locate your teaching style on this theoretical/practical spectrum?

   Very Practical   Very Theoretical

3. _____ is a person of wisdom. His wisdom goes beyond knowledge because

_____

_____

_____

_____

This person maintains a unity of "knowing" and "doing" by

_____

_____

_____

_____

4. What are the dynamics or steps in your teaching style that make it possible for you/for other learners to approach learning in a humanizing way?

5. Rank and discuss in order of importance from very important to least important the dynamics of wisdom education. Also add whatever essential dynamics that you consider missing from this list.

- People are able to see things for themselves.
- People actively use all of their gifts.
- People realize that experience counts.
- People know that even the most mundane data holds the possibility of wisdom.
- People collaborate.
- People are encouraged to reach deep within themselves and draw upon the resources at the core of their being.
- People seek reciprocal relationships.
- People converse openly.
- People think for themselves.

6. How important is it among other curriculum demands to nurture contemplation in the classroom, parish program or family? Is contemplation the highest achievement of education? Explain.

7. For the most part are the learners you work with committed to lifelong learning? What aspects of your teaching style nurture this attitude?

8. I make an effort to help learners cultivate:

a passion for truth by

_____

_____

_____

_____

a passion to do what is true by

_____

_____

_____

_____

a passion to help others do what is true by

_____

_____

_____

_____

_____

◈

_____

_____

_____

_____

_____

_____

_____

_____

_____

_____

Concluding Thought

"Start by doing what's necessary; then do what's possible; and suddenly you are doing the impossible."

—*St. Francis of Assisi*

Write your response to this quote here.

_____

_____

_____

_____

Glossary

cognitive—related to the act of knowing, with an emphasis on the intellect and including both awareness and judgment.

epistemology—the study of the nature of knowledge.

Scholasticism—the dominant philosophical and theological method in western Christianity from the 10th to 17th century.

Enlightenment—a philosophical movement in the 18th century that emphasized rationalism and rejected the authority of traditional social, religious, and political ideas.

CHAPTER SEVEN

A Spirituality for Everyone: "Our Hearts Are Restless. . ."

Recap

The very nature of humanizing education makes it possible for every educator to engage and nurture people as spiritual beings, although most often doing so quite subtly. Of course, spiritual nurturing is readily recognized as a responsibility of parents in the home. Likewise, this is expected of religious educators in parish programs, in every parochial and religiously-affiliated school. But I propose that teachers in any educational context can help "take care of souls," especially by their relationships with learners and by how they teach—even where religious language is excluded. All educators are wise to place a spiritual vision at the foundation of their teaching. (page 324)

In Christian tradition, the *spirit* in *spirituality* is also God's Spirit. The Holy Spirit moves within human spirits to entice us into relationship with God and to allow this primary relationship to permeate all relationships—with self, others, and the world. Christian spirituality, then, is a partnership between God's Spirit and human spirits—working in kinship. Spiritual growth is a lifelong journey, sustained by God's Spirit through our own, into living as a people of God. (page 325)

Our great spiritual reservoir then is the human heart, with all its desires and longings. This means educators are to turn learners toward their interiority, to their own souls. When teachers and parents encourage learners to take seriously and probe their human desires for signals of truth, goodness, and beauty, they foster their spirituality. (page 329)

Note first that spirituality is one's way of life—an aspect in need of emphasis. Spirituality is often made to sound esoteric and removed from life—confined to the interior self rather than lived out in the everyday. Perhaps this is true in some traditions, but from a Christian point of view, our spirituality is realized in how we live our day-by-day lives. (page 330)

Note well that *holiness of life* and *living justly* are equivalent demands of the covenant with God. Both amount to *right relationship*—justice and spirituality are not realized apart from each other. (page 333)

. . . the defining symbol of Jesus' way of holiness is the reign of God—doing God's will of peace and justice, love and compassion, freedom and fullness of life, on earth as it is done in heaven. (page 334)

Teachers and parents simply must care for their own souls. To educate in a humanizing way, it seems imperative that educators pay attention to their interiority and have sources to nourish their own depths, patterns to experience awe and express reverence, practices to cultivate a sense of ultimate value in who they are and what they do in learners' lives. In brief, it will be difficult for teachers and parents to care for learners' souls if they do not take care of their own! (page 346)

For Reflection (60 minutes)

1. Imagine a teacher or parent asking you, "What has spirituality got to do with education?" How would you respond?

2. Review the sources of your own response—autobiographical, social, and otherwise. Do you feel any need for a shift in perspective?

3. Will engaging people as spiritual beings threaten the academic rigor of education? Why or why not?

4. What might it mean for teachers and parents to approach learners as spiritual beings? For the educator's soul? Style? For the teaching/learning environment?

5. Imagine some adjustments that a holistic spirituality might suggest for your own teaching/parenting.

6. Is it too late—or even advisable—for Western education to retrieve its spiritual heritage, to reunite the assets of monastery and university? Take your own position, giving your reasons for or against.

7. How do you imagine your educational environment can be enhanced as a place which nurtures spirituality?

8. Where do you now stand on the issue of the relationship between spirituality and education?

9. Is there a decision emerging for you regarding the spiritual aspect of your own teaching?

Additional Reflections (30 minutes)

*The rest of the story . . .*Recall a story from your experience about a person you know whom you consider an excellent listener. How does good listening nurture your own soul? The souls of others? Truth, beauty, and goodness? Does good listening necessarily change one's perspective?

1. What do you consider core elements of nurturing your own soul? The souls of others?

2. How does spiritual awakening take place in a learning environment? How does your teaching style nurture the spirituality of others? How does it engage the soul?

3. What are the consequences of not engaging the soul of learners? How does loss of soul affect the humanization process?

4. My spiritual vocation is

   _____

   _____

5. Rank on a scale of very important to least important the value you place on these spiritual practices. Also add whatever practices that you find helpful.

   • The need for daily prayer.

   • The value of being part of a faith community.

   • The importance of a soul-friend.

   • Being closer to God through acts of justice and compassion.

   • Giving balance to your life—integrating physical, mental, psychological, and spiritual needs.

   • Reviewing the events of each day with God.

6. If spirituality is one's way of life, what steps do you take in your teaching style to guard against making it esoteric and removed from life?

7. Discuss: Only God can fully satisfy our longings. To neglect our spirituality is to be less than who we are.

8. What in your teaching style/learning environment helps you "to act justly, to love tenderly, and to walk humbly with your God" (Micah 6:8)?

9. Personal prayer and liturgical prayer renew my spiritual life in these key ways

_____

_____

10. Conclude the discussion process by repeating question one in the For Reflection section: What does spirituality have to do with education?

_____

_____

More specifically, how does your teaching style/educational environment engage learners to express their interiority?

_____

_____

To reverence the ordinary and to notice Mystery?

_____

_____

To explore their own depths?

_____

_____

To discern what is good, true, and beautiful?

_____

_____

Concluding Thought

"We belong to God and to one another; this is our deepest identity and noblest vocation."

—Pope John XXIII

What do you think Pope John XXIII would say to you right now about your vocation as teacher/parent to nurture your own soul?

_____

_____

The souls of learners?

_____

_____

Glossary

soul—a person's animating and defining principle, the very life-breath of God in us.

ethos—the distinguishing characteristics, beliefs, and moral core of a person, group, or institution.

spirituality—one's way of life.

CHAPTER EIGHT

A Faith That Does Justice: "Beyond the Scales"

Recap

Any Christian understanding of justice should arise from the Bible and then be complemented by philosophical sources. (page 365)

In the Hebrew Scriptures, the consequence of living in right relationship with God, self, others, and creation is *shalom*. Conversely, shalom is the rule of justice as right relationship. This term, usually translated as "peace," means much more—solidarity among all peoples, harmony with creation, wholeness and complete well-being for everyone, the best of everything that is best for all. (page 367)

In Jesus' life and preaching, his central passion was for *the reign of God*. Likewise, it was the touchstone of his commitment to justice and peace. There is no doubt that God's reign was understood at the time and by Jesus as demanding justice for all. (page 368)

In their own lives, teachers and parents need to have a personal passion for justice. Without "fire in the belly" for justice, educators are less likely to educate others in this "cardinal" virtue . . . . Justice educators must redefine success, becoming convinced that the simplest efforts are worthwhile—that everyone can do something. And the smallest victories should be celebrated. (pages 381–382)

All education is capable of teaching for or against justice, which is to say that education is always "political"! Both the *what* and *how* of education affect who people become and how they live in society—big-time politics!

For Reflection (60 minutes)

1. What is your own basic understanding of "justice"? How did you come by it?

2. Recall a "dangerous memory" that could enhance your commitment to social justice. What does it ask of you personally? As a teacher or parent?

3. From your own experience, can you describe some instances of the interrelation between education and justice? Do some social analysis on one of your examples.

4. What are your own sentiments about the place of justice in your work as an educator? Describe how it belongs. Review some of the personal and social influences on your position.

5. Recall a notable instance when you brought concern for justice to your teaching or parenting. What do you learn from the experience as you reflect on it now?

6. What do you imagine a commitment to justice asks of an educator's soul? Style? Of the educational environment?

7. Has your own understanding of justice and its place in your teaching changed or grown from your encounter with this chapter? How? Why?

8. What would you challenge in this chapter? What insights would you add to it?

9. Can you imagine ways to enhance your own commitment to educate for justice?

Additional Reflections (30 minutes)

The rest of the story . . . Recall a specific situation from your experience that vividly reminds you that your faith demands just actions from you. Jot down and discuss how this experience comforted you.

_____

_____

_____

Disturbed you

_____

_____

_____

1. How do the seven corporal works of mercy permeate the educational environment in your classroom/parish program/home? The seven spiritual works of mercy?

2. What in your teaching style/educational environment encourages learners not only to include but to go beyond in providing others with more than their due?

3. What were the major influences in shaping your conscience? What in your teaching style reflects those influences?

4. In what way does your basic understanding of justice arise from the Bible? What is your memory of the way the Bible was presented to you as a child in your religious education years?

5. What are some classroom tips you can offer to help teachers educate for justice?

_____

_____

_____

_____

6. What are some specific classroom strategies you recommend for each of these dynamics?

• human dignity gives rights and responsibilities

_____

_____

_____

_____

• people have a need to be in community

_____

_____

_____

_____

• justice demands care for the common good, for honesty and fairness, for fair distribution of social goods, for social structures that safeguard human rights

_____

_____

_____

_____

7. What are some examples of how your learners live out the reign of God? In what way is the reign of God the overarching vision your teaching style? The educational environment?

8. Why does good ministry necessarily involve justice?

⊷◈⊶

_____

_____

_____

_____

_____

_____

_____

_____

_____

_____

_____

_____

_____

⊷◈⊶

Concluding Thought

"Injustice anywhere is a threat to justice everywhere."
                                    —*Martin Luther King, Jr.*

Is this a true statement? Why?

_____

_____

_____

The most important aspects of educating for justice are

_____

_____

_____

_____

Glossary

virtue—a quality that becomes part of a person through repeated activity.

shalom—God's promise of peace and well-being for all people and creation.

justice—philosophically, can be described as giving people their due and what they need to live humanly. Basically, justice is to live in "right relationship" with God, self and others.

$\mathscr{A}$ "Catholic" Openness:
"Here Comes Everybody"

Recap

Humankind, at its best, reaches for "catholicity." Our deepest desire is to transcend sectarianism and parochialism and live instead with authentic love of self and others and in solidarity with all people. (page 395)

Catholic Christianity affirms and celebrates particularity—so necessary for personal identity. At its best, it is not an amorphous universalism but *a grounding that opens to the universal.* It should provide deep roots that nurture branches to reach beyond parochialism to inclusivity in care and consciousness. (page 396)

Inclusion and outreach—catholicity—were certainly the spirit of the historical Jesus. He sought out and preached to all classes of society, of every ethnic background. (page 397)

God's universal love lends the mandate to people of God to live likewise—to love without limits and borders. There should never be "us and them" but only "we"—bonded as one human family. (page 401)

On the personal level, no one should despair because of life's difficulties—we always retain our agency and can do something to improve our lot, if only to say "no" to debilitating circumstances. (page 403)

A catholic outlook is open to surprises, to be confronted, to be enriched, to be changed by the entire breadth of human knowledge and wisdom. A catholic perspective is the antithesis of closed-mindedness. It seeks out and welcomes truth regardless of its human sources—because all truth has one divine Source. (page 405)

Being catholic entails an abiding love for all people with commitment to their welfare, rights, and justice. It welcomes human diversity, is open to learn from other traditions, and lives in solidarity with all humankind as brother and sister. A catholic cherishes his/ her particular culture and roots of identity while reaching for an open horizon and a global consciousness. A catholic community is radically inclusive of diverse peoples and perspectives; it is free of discrimination and sectarian sentiment; and welcomes "the stranger" with outreach, especially to those most in need. (page 413)

For Reflection (60 minutes)

1. What are some of your own immediate associations when you hear the term "catholic"? Review their origin.

2. Note some ways in which your faith community is catholic. Ways in which it is not—yet. Reflect on why.

3. What in your social context promotes catholicity? What prevents it?

4. In what ways do you recognize yourself as a catholic educator? Why?

5. Imagine that your school or program or family has decided to make a commitment to a thoroughly catholic education—a truly humanizing one that educates for life for all. Can you suggest a symbol or slogan to help sustain such commitments?

6. What do you think catholicity asks of teachers' or parents' hearts? Of their style? Of the educational space?

7. What do you agree or disagree with in these reflections on catholicity for education and the vocation of educator? Reflect on what brings you to take the positions that you do.

8. What insights or proposals would you add to those here about catholicity and its challenge for teachers and parents?

9. What decisions are emerging for your own teaching/ parenting style and environment in response to the challenge of catholicity?

Additional Reflections (30 minutes)

*The rest of the story . . .*Recall a story from your experience which has helped you to understand the inclusivity and diversity of God's human family. The diversity of God's human family enriches my faith

———————————————————————

———————————————————————

———————————————————————

No matter what the individual differences are, these are the common-denominator hopes of God's human family

———————————————————————

———————————————————————

———————————————————————

1. These are some ways that my teaching style reflects the teaching style of Jesus

   _____

   _____

   _____

   My favorite gospel story about Jesus

   _____

   _____

   _____

2. What are the sources that provide you with hope and a positive sense of the future? How does your teaching style/educational space radiate hope? How do you deal with disappointment and setbacks?

3. For me, being catholic entails

   _____

   _____

   _____

4. Rank in importance from very important to less important the values of catholicity according to the following dynamics. Also add what dynamics you feel are missing.

   • All people are good.

   • There is "more" within the ordinary.

   • To be truly catholic means to be welcoming.

   • To be truly catholic is to honor tradition.

   • The wisdom of the catholic tradition is life-giving.

   • My definition of a school, program or family that is truly catholic is

   _____

   _____

   _____

Of a catholic educator is

_____

_____

_____

Of a catholic learning space

_____

_____

_____

5. What keeps your curiosity and creativity alive? How do you foster creativity and a spirit of curiosity in your learners?

6. What are the essentials in religious education as to shaping religious identity? To avoiding ideologies?

⬥

_____
_____
_____
_____
_____
_____
_____
_____
_____
_____
_____
_____
_____
_____

Concluding Thought

"To live a creative life, we must lose our fear of being wrong."
—*Joseph Chilton Pearce*

What are some factors that foster creativity? Inhibit creativity? In what way does the fear of being wrong make one live less creatively?

_____

_____

_____

_____

Glossary

discipleship—the following of Jesus by men and women of Christian faith.

fundamentalism—movements in any religious tradition who object to critical study of official teachings

covenant—relationship between two or more parties.

CHAPTER TEN

The Vision in Review: "Keeping On" as Educators for Life

Recap

Catholic education engages the human spirit—the soul, the ultimate source of human solidarity—and educates for justice for all. (pages 426–429)

A summary of what each of the eight depth structures of Catholic Christianity suggests for the educator's soul, style, and space will give a cumulative sense of the spiritual vision to teachers and parents . . . .

For the Educator's Soul

. . . an abiding spirit of affirmation, appreciation, and celebration of life and human beings . . . a sense of the "more in the midst" . . . . [to] educate in ways that promote the "common good" . . . . an appreciation of tradition . . . . a deep passion for truth—to pursue it, to live it, to teach it . . . . to become fully alive to the glory of God . . . . a personal passion for justice, [and] openness of mind and heart . . . .

For the Educator's Style

. . . . [to create] communities of participation and conversation . . . . [and to honor] these seven commitments that mark a *for life-for-all* style of teaching . . . engaging, attending, expressing, reflecting, accessing, appropriating, and deciding . . . .

For the Teaching Space

. . . teachers and parents can enhance their educational space in humanizing ways by:

—Helping to build community.

—Welcoming diversity.

—Giving people encouragement.

—Nurturing character.

—Teaching in ways that are just and that help to form learners in living justly.

—Giving opportunities for service .

—Encouraging openness.

—Attending to the aesthetic . . . and nurturing imagination.

—Fostering moral and spiritual formation. (pages 428–440)

For Reflection (60 minutes)

1. Remember a few of your own "saints' in teaching—your "Gussies." What strikes you as most important to take from their modeling of this noble vocation?

2. What are some of your eutopian hopes for your own educating? What aids their realization? What hinders?

3. Name some of the commitments that mark your vocation as educator/parent. How did you come by them?

4. What helps you to "keep on" as a teacher or parent?

5. From you experience as an educator, if you had one piece of advice to give to a beginning teacher or parent, what would it be?

6. What other suggestions would you add to help sustain educators in educating for life?

7. What is the next step in your own spiritual journey as a teacher or parent?

8. With whom would you like to share the spiritual vision that has emerged from your conversation with *Educating for Life?* How will you share it? When?

Additional Reflections (30 minutes)

The rest of the story . . .Make up a short story about a fictional teacher in a fictional school who reveals to his/her students day after day, year after year that "I really love you."

_____

_____

_____

_____

1. What is the most important principle in *Educating for Life* that you want to more fully implement in your teaching/parenting style? Educational space?

2. My spiritual vision of educating *for life for all* is

_____

_____

_____

3. In terms of educating for life, what dynamics seem to be more operative in today's world of education compared to the world of education that I encountered as a child?

_____

_____

_____

The benefits from this trend are

_____

_____

_____

4. In terms of educating for life, what dynamics seem to be less prevalent in today's world of education compared to the world of education that I encountered as a child?

_____

_____

_____

The drawbacks from these trends are

_____

_____

_____

5. I am a *for-life-for all* educator whenever I

_____

_____

_____

6. What are some of the things you need to know about your learners in order to effectively educate for life?

_____

_____

_____

7. Do you think young people have a difficult time communicating with adults? Explain.

_____

_____

_____

What fosters good communication between generations?

_____

_____

_____

What hinders good communication between generations?

_____

_____

8. Rank on a scale from strong to not so strong a character profile of the learners with whom you work Explain the ranking.

   Responsible • Flexible • Practical • Thoughtful • Prayerful • In Touch with the Needs of Others • Trustworthy • Fun to Be With. . . .

   What does this character profile have to do with educating for life?

   _____

   _____

9. What are some of the good things your learners have to give to others?

   _____

   _____

10. The question I want to ask Thomas Groome regarding *Educating for Life* is (you can reach Dr. Groome directly at http://www.RCLweb.com/thomasmore/)

   _____

   _____

   _____

   _____

_____

_____

_____

_____

_____

_____

_____

_____

Concluding Thought

"True saints live in the midst of other people. They rise in the morning. They eat and sleep when needed. They buy and sell in the marketplace just like everyone else. They marry, have children, and meet with their friends. Yet never for an instant do they forget God."

—Abu Sa'id

What is it that enables true saints to never for an instant forget God?

_____

_____

_____

What does educating for life have to do with fostering or nurturing true saints?

_____

_____

_____

_____

Glossary

vocation—from the Latin *vocatus*—calling—the sense that each person has their own particular function to fulfill in life; people of faith see God as the source of their vocation.

communion of saints—the concept that the whole people of God—both living and dead—are bonded as one people by God's Holy Spirit.

For Your Reflection

For Your Reflection

_____
_____
_____
_____
_____
_____
_____
_____
_____
_____
_____
_____
_____
_____
_____
_____
_____
_____
_____
_____
_____
_____
_____
_____
_____
_____
_____
_____
_____
_____
_____
_____

For Your Reflection

_____

_____

_____

_____

_____

_____

_____

_____

_____

_____

_____

_____

_____

_____

_____

_____

_____

_____

_____

_____

_____

_____

_____

_____

_____

_____

_____

_____

_____

For Your Reflection

_____
_____
_____
_____
_____
_____
_____
_____
_____
_____
_____
_____
_____
_____
_____
_____
_____
_____
_____
_____
_____
_____
_____
_____
_____
_____
_____
_____